Look At All The Women

CATHY BRYANT

Also by Cathy Bryant

<u>Solo Poetry Collection</u>:
Contains Strong Language and Scenes of a Sexual Nature (Puppywolf Press 2010)

<u>Co-Editor</u>:
Best of Manchester Poets, Volume 1 (Puppywolf Press 2010)
Best of Manchester Poets, Volume 2 (Puppywolf Press 2011)
Best of Manchester Poets, Volume 3 (Puppywolf Press 2013)

Look At All The Women

CATHY BRYANT

Mother's Milk Books

First published in Great Britain in 2014 by Mother's Milk Books

ISBN 978-0-9573858-2-5

Typeset in Georgia and Desire by Teika Bellamy and Georgie St Clair.
Printed and bound in Great Britain by The Russell Press, Nottingham,
on FSC paper and board sourced from sustainable forests.
www.russellpress.com

First published in 2014 by Mother's Milk Books
www.mothersmilkbooks.com

SPECIAL THANKS TO:

Keir Thomas, Sue Barnard, Rosie Garland,
Teika Bellamy, Angela Topping and Neil Bundy.

ACKNOWLEDGEMENTS

Some of these poems appear in previous publications:

'Take — ' was first published in *Best of Manchester Poets, Volume 3* (Puppywolf 2013). 'The Lure' was first published in *Page & Spine* (February 2014). 'Ticking' was first published in *The Road Less Travelled* (Dagda Publishing 2012). 'Now' and 'Sealove' were first published in *Contains Strong Language and Scenes of a Sexual Nature* (Puppywolf 2010). 'The Biggest Problem' was first published in *Bugged* (Completely Novel 2010). 'Song Necklace' was first published in *Inspired by Tagore* (Sampad 2012). 'Sense in Your Absence' was first published in *Nin* (Volume 1, Issue 2). 'The Honey Times' was first published in *Stonetelling* (Issue 10). 'Skimming Stones' and 'Broken Biscuits' first appeared in *Constellations* (Volume 3, Fall 2013). 'Apple Child' first appeared in *Hyacinth Noir* (Yule 2012). 'When' first appeared in *The Voices Project* (April 2013). 'At Last' and 'Unbreakable' were first published in *Musings on Mothering* (Mother's Milk Books 2012). 'The Alien' was first published in *Futuredaze* (Underwords 2013). 'Gifts of Fruit for Travellers' was first published in *Always Write Again* (March 2012). 'I Want One' was first published in *The Spark* (Selfselfself 2013). 'Mother and Child' was first published in the *Ghana Poetry Prize Anthology* (Ghana Poetry Foundation 2013). 'Child and the Future' was first published on the *Swanezine* website. 'Mars in the Midlands' was first published in *The Great Escape* (October 2012). 'Certain Small Things' was first published in *Heart Shoots* (Indigo Dreams 2013). 'Glen' was first published on *The Rialto* website. 'Wonder at the Change' was first published in *Sein und Werden* (October 2012). 'The Gift of Chin Mu, 2346 BCE' was first published in *Cha* (Issue 22, December 2013). 'Yellow

Roses on Snow' was first published in *Spark — A Creative Anthology Volume III* (Empire & Great Jones Little Press 2013). 'The White Rose' was first published in *She's the One* (MyWorld 2013). 'Works Xmas Do' was first published by *Liverpool Creative Writing* (December 2013). 'The Insecurity of Mislocated Breasts' was first published in *The English Chicago Review (Issue 2)*.

CONTENTS

The Mothers

The Eclectic Others

Introduction and Dedication

"Would you do the 'juh' for 'Janet', please, Cathy? That's the one with a line at the top, and then an umbrella handle underneath. Then next to that you put an eight — that's the two circles one on top of the other, or there's a clever twisty way to do it that I can show you in a minute. Then after the eight put a nought — that's a big oval or circle. Well done!"

This wasn't at school or nursery. Actually I'd flatly refused to go back to nursery school on the grounds that it was too cold and that they wouldn't let me use enough toilet paper (these still seem to be excellent reasons!), and so my parents had decided to save the pound that it cost per week (!) to send me there. So there I was, three years old, at a ten-pin bowling alley with my mother and her friends in the afternoon, in 1971, on the south coast of England. I got to do the scoring, which I was told was very important, and I thoroughly enjoyed it. I didn't realise how momentous it was — that here was a group of friendly women who just happened, in their precious spare time, to be teaching me to write letters and numbers. I was just happily wondering whether the umbrella handle of a 'juh' went left or right, and which was left and which was right anyway.

I remember so many episodes like this from childhood and adulthood — groups of women performing a thousand cheerful kindnesses on a daily basis and helping everyone get by or get on. The bowling alley came to mind when I was wondering about a dedication for this book — there are so many women to whom I wanted to offer it! My sisters-in-law who are lovely, my supportive friends, the English teacher who took risks and got us to read 'Daddy' by Sylvia Plath at school, the woman in hospital who, when I came on unexpectedly and burst into tears, offered me her last pair of clean knickers (greater love hath no woman than that she shall lay down her last pair of knickers for a stranger's sake...), the poetry editor who is willing to publish a full collection of my poetry during a recession, and a thousand more.

Some of them feature in this book — the never-sufficiently-thanked dinner ladies, for example. But I've played with language, ideas and form as I like to do, so you'll also find women from the myths of ancient Greece, Europe and Africa, and they'll all have their say in different forms, whether villanelle, sonnet, free verse or list poetry. Some struggle, and some are having great sex and a laugh. Some of them are me, and many are not.

I couldn't pick out one or two women for the dedication, so this collection is gratefully offered to all the women in the world who help out their fellow humans, usually without much in the way of pay or recognition. Thank you. I wouldn't have made it this far without you. I've even mastered that twisty 8 now.

Cathy Bryant, Spring 2014

Editor's Note

When Cathy submitted her poem 'Unbreakable' for inclusion in the anthology *Musings on Mothering* I wondered at how she'd managed to so perfectly describe my own feelings about mothering through breastfeeding. *She's been there*, I thought.

Except she hadn't, which I later discovered, after keeping a beady eye on her poetry career.

This made 'Unbreakable' all the more remarkable and highlighted Cathy's skill in utilising one of the most important traits of an accomplished poet — empathy. What Cathy had done was watch and listen with the eyes and ears of a poet; she had made note of the often overlooked interactions between mothers and their children, the everyday tendernesses which build their relationships, and stepped into the shoes of a mother or two, or three. She walked around in their shoes for a bit, probably got comfy, and then composed a breathtakingly beautiful poem.

I am a fan of the eclectic and admire writers who skillfully handle the differing requirements of poetry and prose, experimenting with differing themes and writing in various genres. Cathy is one such writer, so I was very pleased indeed to learn a while ago that she had a poetry collection in search of a publisher...

Cathy's manuscript was everything I expected it to be: joyous, laugh-out-loud funny, passionate and thought-provoking. I admit that some of the poems: 'Caleb Hollow's Room', 'Rape Rack', 'The White Rose' and 'Rape Dreams in the Slush Pile' upset me because I'd prefer to live in a world without so many shades of darkness. Yet I am glad that Cathy sheds light on these terrible things because we are in dire need of brave souls to illuminate dark terrain and help us to navigate a way through it.

Cathy is adept at switching from dark to light — with an especial talent for poking fun at prim (and very British) sensibilities towards romance and sex, telling us of 'Sexual Positions for Those No Longer Young' and 'What the Sirens Sang To Odysseus' and recounting, with great charm, what 'The Biggest Problem' may be for a couple on a train.

Mostly though, Cathy reminds us to 'Look At All The Women' and to delight, indeed, bathe in all their multicoloured glory, for: 'What a waste of time / life would be without them.'

Teika Bellamy, Spring 2014

The Lovers

Pistachios

Splitting pistachio shells he hogs
the eau-de-nil kernels with their pale tang,
throwing the husks to pistol-shot in the fire.

Her question hasn't been answered.
The air is taut with salt and desire,
roasting in cracked nuts and the movements
of his silent mouth.

She draws her hand through the unbroken nut heap
as she might trail it in the translucent mystery
of a river, soft with weeds, in a dream;
then clenches a fist on small hardnesses,
remembering open spaces.

The fire doesn't give a damn about any of this.
It rumbles on, delighted by its own voice,
like the "marvellous character" at the pub,
whisky handed, telling his old sexist jokes.

Dour rusted men shouldn't eat pistachios.
Their women should ignore the unspoken
verdict, make a run for it into sunshine
and lick green ice cream, licking, licking, licking,
lapping and flicking with the whole of the tongue.

Unromance Unveiled

(with apologies to Plath, Zonas, Byron, T'ing Yun, Waller,
Tennyson, Shakespeare, Amichai and Millay)

Love set you going like a fat gold watch;
now you're overwound and drink too much Scotch.

A pomegranate just splitting, a peach just furry,
are enticing. But you, my dear ex, are just slurry.

She walks in beauty, like the night.
In daylight she's a sorry sight.

In the moonlit chamber, always she thinks of him;
he too makes her claustrophobic, he too is dim.

Go, lovely Rose, and tell her that wastes her time and mine
— hell, I'm talking to a flower. I've had too much wine.

Now lies the Earth all Danaë to the stars
while we drink lager in late licence bars.

When shall we three meet again?
Blind drunk on the late night train.

The end was quick and bitter —
the other bloke was fitter.

What lips my lips have kissed, and where, and why,
will no doubt be on Facebook by and by.

Smoke and Mirrors

They do it with mirrors, I was always told
when my eyes grew round at the magic;
it's simple conjuring and can all be explained.
Unlike love — and I fell for the magician,
as hard as the entwined steel rings and as deep
as the inside of a pupil-black top hat.
But soon I was weary of posing in leotards,
with sequins, spangles and teeth sparkling,
hand pointing to the tricks while my damned
outfit crawled up my bottom and disappeared.
All the glory was his as he lifted rabbits,
those poor drugged rabbits, out by the ears
or sawed me (smiling all the while) in half,
or showed great delight in making me invisible.
By now the bond between us was no more
than a tatty string of motley-coloured cloths,
and all I felt was relief when his acts were over
and finally he vanished, forever, in a puff of smoke.

Dinner Invitation*

He asked me out to eat a meal.
I pictured silver forks, red wine.
I got poshed up in dress and heels.
He asked me out to eat a meal.
Our eating place was then revealed:
'Forton Services' said the sign.
He asked me out, to eat a meal.
I pictured silver forks, red wine...

* This is a true story — he even talked me through the menu, explaining which were the items that gave the best value for money! I'll leave it to your imagination whether or not there was a second date. For American readers — Motorway Services are the equivalent of your Truck Stops.

Brid, December

Bold gemini moon full on
and the waves fly up to meet it.
The sea stirs; every last creature
swims or wriggles up to drink
the light, taste the moon's essence.

A streetlamp bravely does its best.
Oi! Look at me! Regard! I shine too!
It gets in the way, spoiling photos.
Vampires and tourists slink off in disgust.

Lovers ignore it. The moon, the sea,
each other — there's nothing else
but warm, clean-sheeted beds.
Light is light, isn't it?

No. You could skim the silver
from the waves with one hand,
and make your face holy with it,
immortal.

Take —

An exam. Ages to get ready. Sugar in tea.
An interest. A chance. Your clothes off. Virginity.
The long view. Me as your lawful wedded.
This ring. Vows. The last slice of cake.
Us as you find us. Each day as it comes.
Your time.
Offence. The piss. Umbrage.
No prisoners. Hostages.
That. It on the chin.
Pains.
My advice. Two tablets every four hours.
A chair. Five. Time out. A deep breath.
A minute to calm down. A moment to reflect.
Out. Some time off. A break. It from me.
It one day at a time. It easy. Away.
Lessons in a foreign language. A holiday.
Flight.
My breath away. Care. A lover. Me as I am.
A mental photograph of you smiling.
My hand. Pleasure in it. Heart.

The Lure

I know he's a rascal. I know he's a rat,
seducing with charm and a raise of his hat;
making off with the jewels of every countess
and then living a life of quite splendid excess.
I mustn't allow him my love nor my cash —
but he has such a devilish, handsome moustache.

He'll cheat you at cards, he'll cheat at the races
cheat damsels of trust and then leave with no traces.
He'll charm anyone with his wit and his face,
with his twinkling eyes and his debonair grace.
I shouldn't allow him my love nor my cash,
but he has such a devilish, handsome moustache.

I gave him my money, I gave him my heart.
He took them, and told me that we'd never part
and then left within minutes of promising bliss
but I've not a regret, not for even a kiss.
Though my money's all gone and my hopes are now ash,
he had such, *such* a devilish, handsome moustache.

Sleeping with Paul Darrow

One day I will sleep with Paul Darrow,
back when he was in his 30s, about Blake's 7 time.
One day I will live by the sea again,
which is like falling in love for the first time every day.
One day I will see a seal in the sea.
One day my beloved will let me teach him to waltz,
and we'll spiral the garden by moonlight.
One day I will sleep with Paul Darrow (as Avon) and hear
cynical endearments in syruped gravel.
Ditto (with the sleeping bit) Debbie Harry, Jacqueline Bisset,
Kate Bush, Harrison Ford, Tom Baker and Joan Greenwood.
One day I will spend a week doing nothing.
One day I will wear a ballgown on the moon.
One day I will give birth to a litter of kittens.
One day I will sing more than a snatch of song onstage,
and I will not joke about it afterwards.
One day I will sell everything I own, give the money away
and have the courage to live on nothing,
and not mind when it goes horribly wrong.
One day I will have a conversation with a constellation,
and hear the sounds that stars make when they laugh and cry.
One day I will become a bell, a dream or a book.
One day I will save someone or something.
One day I will see the Aurora Borealis with Paul Darrow.
I don't really care what age he is.
One day. Though, quite frankly, wanting these thing is
wonderful and warming enough, without doing them.
Dreams are too delightful to put aside.
See you soon, Paul. Wear the black.

Ticking

You sometimes have to shake it, to make it go,
the watch that he gave to me as a love gift.
He gave it to me seventeen years ago;
you sometimes have to shake it to make it go.
He died, and soon both I and watch will follow
to mysterious chasms, the darkling rift.
You sometimes have to shake it to make it go,
the watch that he gave to me as a love gift.

Now

Utterly defeated,
pessimism took its mortal wound today.
'I'm only going to say this once,' you said,
and then said what you said;
annihilating insecurity, low self-esteem,
the voice that whispers 'no hope'
— all silenced.

Not only love but also a sacrifice
that as you offered it to me broke over you
and you wept in tidal waves
while I bloomed in a swift time-lapse
out of tight-fist-bud
into open-hand-flower.

Unasked you gave me everything.
That sound you can hear
is a new adult weeping
at the astonishing, near-unbelievable gift
that is you.
I now know that you love me.
I shall stop fearing joy, now.

Still Life

He is primed and ready for love's sketches,
the gouache young Phthalo, and he scumbles
at first sight of the Lady Fauve by the lake.
She sits, calmly drinks chiaroscuro, keeping
her tempura even as Lord Turpentine umbers
clumsy compliments. To her all men are pastels.
Her palette demands more viridian fare.
To Phthalo she is monestial, and his cousin
Sienna's face falls as she sees him fall deep
into ultramarine feelings; she leaves, pointillist
and watercolour, and rushes off to acrylic.
Fauve looks up, sees Phthalo and loses all
perspective in a flash. Her colours are worked up,
her landscape washed with folly. She raises
her fan brush, but too late: evil Count Alizarin
has noticed the nude chrome of emotion,
and his cruel revenge will be vermillion
and representative.

The Biggest Problem

Crowded carriage,
the usual uncomfortable swaying.
Clutching each other amid strangers.
She turns to him:
'Do you realise what the biggest problem
in our relationship is?'
Oh darling, so not the time nor the place,
say so many faces, wary, worldly,
but also wondering what his answer is
and whether it's what she thought;
and we wait, while he squirms and shifts
and the train goes thunketa-*thun*keta
and the people sniff and cough.
'Well,' he replies, 'Given that everyone here can hear us —
I'm going to say my inadequate penis size.'
— and a great laugh breaks from her,
and the whole carriage smiles
as if it had filled with balloons and cake and friends.
'Actually,' she says lovingly, confidingly,
'It's your cat allergy.
But I think we'll find a way to cope.'
And you can see the pink hearts floating around them,
and the train goes thunketa-*thun*keta
rolling cheerfully on.

Sacrament

He holds my bare feet to warm them
and I remember foot-washings and anointings
in the Bible; did they dip their heads
as you do, beloved, soft hair falling forward,
brushing exposed ankles?

You taught me the song of Solomon,
beloved husband, and silently we sing;
mouths, tongues fruit ripe to bursting.
Credo. This is an act of belief,
of us erased yet also magnified.

Transformed, we are sacred gifts,
velvet made hard, flesh made fluid,
love an incense on our quickened breath
as we cry affirmations: in this moment
a harvest, a thought, a crown of stars
— infinity and eternity in a drop of sweat.

Song Necklace

(for Rabindranath Tagore)

I pick up my necklace of songs
and place it round my neck;
a neck imperfect, caught in time
and lined with it, unlike the songs
and the poems, which live on,
as unending and perfect as love.
And kissing each song like a tear
or a crystal, a precious stone or moment,
I remember and feel again
the love that has never, can never
leave nor fade nor numb.

The tears of farewell fill
my old cracked cup; tears pouring
an ocean of love at my feet, cupped
tears that reflect stars and the endless
stream of the universe, the cup
freshened eternally at the ever-giving
fount; and to all who wept and wrote
and sang, who made their gitanjali,
the loved one drinks in life divine
and whispers a soft, unasked-for
"thank you".

You gave all things, from ancient tales
to new and future memories, my love
who adds new songs to my necklace;
never accepting for me the tawdry
or finite jewellery. You teach me
the yes of clouds that colour sunsets,

of open smiles. For the gifts and teaching,
your gora says, "thank you",
communing in ceaseless renewal.
The necklace is shared out, and grows
now and for all time and beyond time.

(Notes: Gitanjali: song offerings. Gora: fair-faced)

Getting on With It, Romantically Speaking

What do I want to say to you,
my flawed messy love,
my soulmate whom I *could* live without?
I could even find someone else
after you died, and be happy, in time.
So I'll make no pledges to an eternity
none of us really understand anyway;
I shan't drag in moons and stars
nor suns and dust.
Just that — both living,
and happening to find each other
in the same place and time,
we live best together,
better than either could have hoped.
Just that in my jaded self
something moves with simple joy at your touch.
My inner adolescent gasps at your eyes
or smile or voice, from time to time,
among all the everyday,
un-heart-stopping stuff.
Any other life arrangement
would be settling for something,
making do, being realistic
and boringly post-modern.
So let's stay unfashionably faithful
and together, and love and trust,
because it's the right thing to do,
and the alternative a lesser thing.

Dear William

It's not just the plums.
You are so plainly
a selfish man

living in the moment
the personal moment
all for yourself.

The divorce papers
are in the post.
This feels so sweet
and deliciously cold.

Meteors on Cloudy Nights

That's love, isn't it?
When you go to watch meteor showers
in soggy sandwiched clouds, thickly spread
with drizzle, and you drive out at midnight
and never mind work in the morning.

So I take him to Squirrels' Jump, and we see bats,
and Manchester grinning away in lights across from us,
and we sit on the bench and talk rubbish,
cheerful as anything.

Then he takes me to a Derbyshire peak,
and we can't see a thing and it's windy enough
to dry washing in an hour or blow it to China
and we giggle at ourselves, joyfully silly.

There's a gap in the clouds and we gaze
and talk more nonsense until we think,
we *think* we both saw one, anyway we're
so happy that it doesn't matter, and we go home
wet and muddy and knackered and sleep in a heap
and for those short early days there are shooting stars
everywhere, in the fridge and on the windowsill
and in each other's eyes, and it's all delirious.

As it dies, a meteor blazes for less than a second
— but not in the memories of those who saw it.
That bright raised eyebrow will always shoot
and spark. A moment is only a moment at the time.
Remembered, it lasts for life.

Sense in Your Absence

The sight of sky-lithe migrant birds
the sudden kiss of doughnut jam
the laughing burn of snowball *whump*
the heavy drift of velvet drapes
the sound of sweet, far carolling
the faintest touch-too-hot foam bath
the sucked white flesh of artichokes
Remembering in tender shocks:
the touch, by God, the touch of you.

What the Sirens Sang to Odysseus

You have the biggest penis we've ever seen.
We have meat, but someone needs to light the barbecue.
We don't like intelligent, feminist men.
We like muscly adventurers with beard,
tunic and sandals. Such a hot look.
You're so adventurous! Talk to us about yourself.
You'd be the only man here.
Who cares about your wife?
We're just begging for it.
We're all virgins.
We have beer.

Sexual Positions for Those No Longer Young

Too old, too old for reverse cowgirl
or anything with the word 'donkey' in it
except for The Ambling Blackpooler.

We make up our own dances for the divans:
The Upturned Mouse, The Irish Potato
(a mass of pale blemished flesh, I guess),
The Half-full Cup of Tea, The Tipsy Llama;
The Sideways Organ-grinder, and this time
it's *your* turn to be the monkey.

They mustn't sound like cocktails or perfumes
— the Tom Jones Semitone, for instance.
Stick to The Chuckle Brothers Cha Cha Cha,
Getting Right Into the Corners
(an important one, that),
The Disgruntled Librarian, The Belgium.

Darling, let's try Servicing the Caravan,
Polishing the Bevelled Edge, The Newt,
The Plumber's Lunch Break, The Mothy Woollen,
The Tiptoe Tremble with Tray,
The Assembly Instructions in Japanese;

The Summer Pudding, The Slip-on Shoe,
The Countdown Conundrum,
The Saggy Bagpuss Squish, The Torvill & Dean,
The Reconditioned Hoover.
Together we'll write The Saga Sutra.

The Honey Times

Everyone tells you about decay
in harsh chopping strokes, words
like arthritis, ugliness, cancer, chronic pain;
or wrap it up in 'wisdom' and 'parchment wrinkles'.
But no one mentions peace and joy.
A comfortable silence
where once your demons howled — forever,
or so you thought. A flower garden grown
in your heart where, once, broken concrete
displayed the bootings and sprayings of vandals.
The warmth of two fat loving bodies
that would horrify the young judgemental self
— that sensuality of cellulite, of shapes at last
relaxed and fallen, drooping, pollen-heavy.
No one tells you that despite decay,
yes, and illness and pain,
you will know yourself and find ways
to sate your deepest needs; will let yourself
be happy in a home of your own making.
No one tells you of the vivacity, the furious
bee-life fermented into that of the
honey-eater. The sweetness. The plenitude.

The Mothers

Skimming Moments

Mummy, where do ripples come from?

From the stone pushing the water, darling.

And where do the ripples go when they stop?
And where did I come from?

You remember then that because of the most
extraordinary concatenation of circumstances
you looked up and he looked up and your hearts
gave a lurch and somewhere a butterfly flapped
its wings like a beating heart and that's
how typhoons start and children get born.

You squeeze your daughter's hand and wonder
how to explain chance, love, biology, mathematics,
loss. You smile helplessly, sadly at her
and she laughs back and dances.

Apple Child

She was picking apples when she cried out
and felt a warm fluid on her leg,
and a clenching inside. Her basket fell
and she leant back against the tree,
slowly slithering to the earth as contractions came.
Short hours later her love-sister, sensing something,
raced through the fields to the orchard,
her hair streaming, and saw the new mother,
each hand in a fist round a windfall apple
against the pain, back supported by
the good solid trunk. The new baby keened
a little, then gurgled at the earth-sweet scent
of apple trees; slept, warmed to cidrous drowsiness
by the pink and heavy gold of sunset, and the joy
of all kinds of harvest and homecoming.

When

When you know the time to be strong
and when to give way to your feelings;
when you will stand up for yourself
as others blame you unfairly, yet
still be tolerant of different views;
when you can meet triumph and disaster
and know to celebrate one and mourn the other,
because otherwise you'd be a ridiculous
unfeeling rock and your life pointless;
when you know better than to risk all
your life's winnings on a single bet;
when you know that your will is one
of many, all deserving equal respect;
when you can listen in and to crowds, and not
lose the common touch when with royalty;
when you allow people close enough to hurt
you and know your vulnerability, know you;
when you truly love the planet and those in it,
despite the hatred and mocking laughter,
then you will have truly grown up —
and then, you'll be a Woman, my daughter.

At Last

She feeds her baby
and it is the first loving touch
she has ever felt
in her bruised and battered life.
She strengthens and nourishes
her little one,
and introduces him to love and trust
and he does the same for her.
He thrives, and so does she,
for the first time;
for the first time, and forever.

Calling

Phoning my daughter
who is on another continent
is like talking to an alien.
I take refuge in the clichés of panic:
Is the food OK?
Yes, she says. How's the new mum?
I look in the corner at the proud queen.
Doing great, I say, and all five kits too.
Their eyes are still shut.
So what's your room like?
Fine, she says.
Are you OK? I ask.
Yes! She says.
She doesn't ask if I'm OK.
We both know how I am.
So what colour are they?
Are what? I ask.
The kittens! Same as Marmite?
One is, I say, but two are ginger,
two calico. Real mongrel moggies.
Darling, you can come home any time.
Mum! She says. I'm fine!
I know, I lie. I love you.
Yeah, love you too. I have to go.
She's gone and I can't help
some weak foolish tears.
It takes a while to calm down
though watching Marmite helps:
her perfect self-assurance
with the tiny squeaking fluffballs,

her hypnotic tongue, patiently
licking, licking, licking, licking
as if it need never end.

Broken Biscuits

She'd bring home great heavy boxes
of broken biscuits she'd got cheap;
in each box, one or two unblemished circles
or unchipped wafers — unlicensed perfection
that had crept in.

These prizes rounded our eyes with excitement:
the joy of *extra*, of *not supposed to happen*.
So much more delicious than ordinary biscuits,
whose flawlessness was merely expected uniformity.

Mum tried to appear unbroken, could conjure
appearances out of anything, out of nothing.
We believed in her intactness until
we grew too old for biscuits,
brushing the crumbs from our faces.

But we saw her crumbled too often,
fallen on tables, soggy at the edges,
dunked in too much gin. It took time
to realise that the biscuits weren't really that heavy
— that wasn't why she staggered.

We'd put the kettle on then, and sit her down,
try to comfort with a cup of tea, and the familiar
shape and sweetness of a Nice or Marie
pressed gently, hopefully, into her palm.

Declarations

Two nations war in the playroom.
The screams of the wounded draw me
and I have to be the UN, or God.
The history of the war unfolds,
who started it disputed in shrill propaganda,
weapon-toys snatched back up
as hostilities resume —
but I speak firmly, authoritatively,
pretending an adulthood I do not feel
and make arbitrary decisions,
threats and promises,
exhort both sides to be good and get on.
At least this time there was no blood,
the unthinkable blood of my children.
Above all they must survive.
Above all they must not go to war.
Above all they must not, not not
be breakable, mortal.
I would go to war to prevent that.

The Alien

I came upon her as she quivered,
which is their way of crying,
and I asked what was wrong.
She looked at me, shivered
and told me about it, sighing
in their strange language of song.
She explained in silvery notes
that her fur was far too short,
her foot-scales too small, her throat-noise
inconsistently modulated. Motes
like tears fell from her, and I was caught
by the euphony of her voice,
and the beauty of her physical being;
yet she feared that she would never mate.
Felt ugly, put together badly.
So I realised what I was seeing:
an unhappy teenager, full of self-hate;
some things are universal, sadly.
And I hugged her in silent language
as the stars shone coldly down,
and I wished for more love for them all,
the young ones so messed up, so savage
with themselves, like me, too fat, too brown,
or her, feeling adulthood's difficult call.

Influenza, 1918

We made our children smoke
as much as they could,
to kill the germs, as advised.
We did our best.

Faith is four, a war child
and coughing like cannon.
She couldn't smoke much.

What gods saw us in black
and weeping, and thought,
you do not suffer enough?
Fifty million dead so far.

Faith lies as if gassed,
cheeks poppy-red with fever,
lungs filling with mud,
barbed wire through my heart.

Caleb Hollow's Room*

So your child is dead.
To you it may be 'his' room
but it is classed as a spare.
You need to enclose a doctor's letter
as proof of grief. There is nowhere
on the form for your tears.

There is a penalty for under-occupation.
On the first anniversary of his death
you must commence payments.
Look, it's only £13 per week,
or you could always move.

We can assist you with advice.
You do not need room for his possessions now
— they are not essential. Keep one jumper,
maybe, to hold and smell, to cry into,
or small things — his toothbrush, photographs.

We're all downsizing, you know.
We understand your concerns.
What more do you want?

*This poem was written as a response to the news story
about a family asked to pay Bedroom Tax from the first
anniversary of their 11-year-old son's death.*

Rape Rack

"The livestock sector is a major player, responsible for 18 percent of greenhouse gas emissions measured in CO2 equivalent. This is a higher share than transport." (Transport causes 13.5%) — The United Nations FAO

It's a giggle, really — the world destroyed
by the farts of livestock.
You could see it as revenge for the years
in cramped pens, with their kids murdered;
or revenge for the rape rack of artificial insemination
— that's what the farmers call it, they do like a laugh
— the rape rack, with the cow splayed and tethered.
The farmers call it that for fun.

Or it could be revenge for the nubs and cysts
sliced off udders, which are breasts, without anaesthetic,
because they don't quite fit the milking machines.
Or revenge for the newborn calf killed instantly,
or even cut out of the cow in labour, to get
that wonderful butter-soft leather and suede.
But animals don't do revenge.

So the planet suffocates like a battery hen,
like a sick pig dying in its own faeces,
because soy, oat and rice milk don't taste
quite the same, and vegan shoes are a bit pricey;
and you could say that the joke's on us
except that, contrary to the proverb, we can
and are taking it with us.

Gifts of Fruit for Travellers

My niece hands me some purpling plums
before the last awkward goodbye
as I set off with brothers, mums
to leave; to emigrate; to fly.
And as the plane parts shriek and grind
then settle to a steady hum
I don sunglasses, draw the blind
and so the first tears start to come.
But when I land I find swift peace
though somewhere alien — other
— for there a girl, much like my niece,
gives persimmons to her mother.

I Want One

Some facet of brakes or wheels strikes sparks
from the cobbles and the boy whoops and laughs
as his mother bumps the wheelchair along.
"Like a fairground ride!" she beams at me
and I smile back, doing my crutches-waltz
over the uneven stones, each unique like faces
or fingerprints, and the gentle moss between.

The sound and feel of crutch and feet:
clack-thud on the cobbles, silent softness
on moss, transmitted up to my arms.
The wheelchair sounds like a zipwire or train.

A girl, about six, is being dragged along by
her mother, her little legs reluctant. She looks
at the wheeling laughing boy in his sparking
chariot and tugs at her mother's hand: "Mum!
Look, Mum! See that? I want one! I want one!"

Reminder From a Non-octopus

If I could be an octopus
with eight strong suckered arms,
I'd play and clean and dust and fuss
and tidy your toy farms.
I'd bake fresh cakes and never moan
and not a task I'd shirk;
and when I'd washed and wiped and sewn
I'd go out to more work.

My child, I would be proficient
— but I have just two hands.
Octopuses are efficient
— but they can't live on land.
I'm here, and rarely take a rest;
remember, when life's tough:
I love you and I do my best,
so let that be enough.

Unbreakable

Hard to believe now
that we are such separate beings —
you a great strapping
toddler of three, all-knowing,
I a hopeful extemporising
mother.
Thankfully, when you were born
and we parted for the first time,
we kept that close touch.
Feeding fed us both
with love and care
and slowly, only when ready,
you drew away to other
sources of nourishment.
But the everyday miracle
is still there in my memory
of the closeness between us
and of us and in us
and the sweetest, most gentle
bonds are unbreakable.

Mother and Child

Mother, O Mother, the moon has gone out!
Oh no, child, oh no — she will soon be back.
She is waking from sleep and her face stirs,
and then you shall see the whites of her eyes.

That naughty Anansi has spun cobwebs
to cover over the face of the moon;
but the moon smiles and blows off the dream-threads.
Soon she will wake and we will all be bright.
Do not believe that all is trickery.
The moon is honest and magnificent.
You have to believe in what you can see.

The new moon, Mother, the new moon has come!
Like an eyelid, so slowly opening.
Have you seen her, Mother, have you seen her?
Yes, my child, I can see you both shining.

Note: Anansi is the trickster god of West African myth. He often appears in the form of a spider.

Child and the Future

Little one, your hurts, though deep, are fleeting.
You always hope for better, tomorrow.
Not like me, too knowing, slug heart beating
while yours pounds swiftly in joy or sorrow.
As the doors of dreams slam finally shut
and knee grazes become heart's dragging wounds,
one copes with haircut, pay cut, paper cut;
music no longer magic, just nice sounds,
It's not all bad. You keep some illusions.
The drawn-out years become flashing seasons.
You can smile at popular delusions
and settle with your comfortable reasons.
Yet, child of mine, keep hope for better things.
Innocence should shape what the future brings.

The Eclectic Others

Dinner Ladies

What strikes me now is the ingratitude
for the daily square meal
— the endless hummocks of mashed potato,
the phalanxes of cabbage.

At five you don't know
that porridgy tights and lumpen shoes
mean the wearer is in pain
and living with it.

How we made faces at sweet semolina
or sago puddings with their blobs
of warm jam in the middle.
How we moaned at a stringy bit of meat
or a too-thin gravy. We knew nothing
of budgets, of time, of bad equipment.

So many hot, filling platefuls
dished up by the Elsies and Dorises
and Jeans and Peggys, and I remember
their laughter and friendliness
as we took our dirty crockery to them.

They seemed to have it so easy,
like all grown-ups — no school for them.
I just wish that I could remember
saying, "Thank you," more often.

Mars in the Midlands

Bruising thighs on table corners
racing to get to the bathroom
before the others in the morning
— a tangle scramble of limbs voices
arguing radios playing cosy house
full to bursting point look what
a mess a massive pile of dirty
dishes schoolbags coats shoes
all simple stuff jamming with
coughs clothes movements

— later, in a rare moment, she
revels in the sense of quiet,
luxuriating in the delicious fragile
solitude. She can hear a faint
rustle as she turns a page. She
sighs inside at Bradbury's vision
of bleak Martian wastes, wonders
why he keeps using the word
'lonely' when it sounds so perfect,
is wistful for sad spreading planets.

Brontë Country

The sign says, quite simply, 'Brontë Country'
as if we're hunting Brontës
— or perhaps they are about to attack
with wild war whoops and tomahawks
(no coward souls theirs).
Beware of the Brontë.
Do not open your car windows.
Brontës may look cute
but they can take off your hand
with one slash of their jaws,
crinolines thrashing to and fro.
'Wuthering' means 'man-eating'.
'Villette' is a type of garrotte.
The moors are treacherous.
People have died there.
No one lives past forty.

Victory in the Louvre

Looking for Mona — you know which Mona
— and wandering past a genius there, history there,
all regarded with vague unlettered appreciation,
I gazed up a fine staircase and
— WHAM! There she stands. Victory!
The Winged Victory of Samothrace (at the time I
have no idea that's who she is, but what a name!).
Great classical wings and a warrior stance
— one can feel the wind and the armies.
Her stillness is sudden. She has stopped
only to cup her mouth with her right hand
and cry, "Victory! Victory! Victory!"

Poor Nike. Hand, mouth, whole head, arms
long gone; one in a drawer in Germany,
one in a box display by the statue,
and much good that does her.
Not a hint of Ozymandias, though
— she's still supreme in Parian marble,
above callow metaphors of headless generals,
mindless war, losing one's head.
She is fractured but unbowed.
Her muscular cry has thundered up and down
our minds since two hundred years before
Christ was born.

She shouted the joy of victorious Rhodes
and I'm not the first since then to fall for her
and reach willingly for my sword.
In 1939 some other fragments of history,

moustachioed and bereted, carried her to safety,
discretion being the better part of survival, then.
She outlived Hitler, and will outlive me.

Finally I walk away, off to find La Giaconda,
the Mona Lisa. There's a crowd.
An American woman is being a cliché:
"It's so small!" She is as loud and angry
as sport. "No one told me it was so small!"
She feels cheated, you can see.
I say to her, "Try the Winged Victory,"
and then lose myself in the dimensions
of another unconquerable female.

Certain Small Things

Certain small things —
a way of laughing
like yours, quick and wry.
A Moomin mug.
Mauve woollen hand-knits.
Self deprecation.
White wine. Secret tears.
Quirky books, swift temper,
— some of them slip away
on oblivious nights or
busy afternoons.
Was it coffee you liked, or tea?
What colour were your eyes?
Why do some deaths touch
so much more than others,
yet details blur?
In guilt and grief
it's time to recall the list,
the litany of small things
still binding, still true.
The way you bit into cake.
Your silent offering of your heart.
A brown top with
a plunge neckline you wore
with a bold necklace
and your hair up.
Bravery. Some sort of stew.
Not liking to eat fruit.
The laughs we had
when you were at chemo.

A loathing of artsy fartsyness.
You were one of those who
quietly clear up at the end of things.
A blanket. A scarf. Your name.

In remembrance of Sarah Richards

Glen

You comb your hair with thistles and drink at the burn
while the snow-hare is running. The witch appears
as trees do from mist, offers you a warm egg and
a hearth. She is half-here as a damselfly, threadbare
as the skittering clouds. Take the moths from her hair,
and the spiders; lay them gently in alder, to winter.

After the snowmelt runs and the bog softens, squelching
up to the softest skin between the toes, you will stroke,
for a summer moment, the living antlers of a pool-eyed
young stag, and feel them warm and furred. Lice dance
on them, black as the snake-sized benign slugs who
seep out of the bracken at night, while you, naked,
walk into a water-moon. You, glaistrig, green woman
who hears insect wings and washes in waterfalls,
will hold herbs and the young deer will leave a warm
lick on your hand, barter for the fistful of watermint.

Here is the Highland fist of tongue-rough, tongue-smooth
rock. Each stone a fingerprint, a map of whorls like
those rippling on a wild goat's pelt, spelled out in all
colours of moss and time, and each rock, stone, goat
and moss a solace. You remember the living touch
of a long-ago cat, ash coloured and softer than antlers;
you feel the sombre power of mountains. You shift
your feet, toes curling into turf, and cannot say goodbye.
When you drink from that burn and wash off your
weeping, as the hare runs, you will lift your face
and in your hair will be a crown of weed and the
coin of a water-snail, grey as your rain-eyes.

Petrified

Wedding night, and she creeps with her candle
to the chamber, she dressed in new linen,
pale flesh soft and freshly washed.
One nervous hand shakes a little, clutching
the thick smooth stem of a heavy candle,
the other cupping the candleholder.
She is frightened in her ribbons and lace,
opens the chamber door with her heart beating
against her bodice as if trying to escape.
The door opens and she takes in the sight,
stands, like so many victims, frozen in trauma.
She will blame herself later for her stillness,
as most do; curse herself for inaction,
but she didn't know what it meant at first —
her husband lying so still and peaceful-seeming
beneath a gleaming womanly form. The bride
cries out and lets the candle fall, light guttering
as the strange woman's head begins to turn.
The bride just sees the swaying snakes of hair,
the glaring glint of eyes, petrifying even in profile,
and knows her husband for what she always
secretly feared: a cold hard lump of stone,
grotesque as a gargoyle. Before the gorgon turns
its gaze fully on her, the candle goes out and she runs,
she runs, she runs, having seen enough not to kill
but to cool and make her brittle; a blanched bride
embarking on a new life of grey blankness
amid terrible whispers and stony stares.

Vomitarium/Nebula

I remember about ten Latin words.
The vomitarium was where Romans
threw up in order to eat more.
"Atrium means hall," said my Latin teacher;
"Penetralium means — " which reminded me
that I had slept with his brother, a hairy
bassist, the week before.
The teacher was probably the nicer of
the two; the bassist was a surly fuck 'n' run.
"Nebula," persisted the teacher ad infinitum
(oh look, I do know more Latin words!)
"What does it mean? What does it sound like?"
"It sounds like nebula. Does it mean nebula?"
That's me asking, cheeky-cocky-cute. My life
is a mucky mess of crap interspersed with
bad jokes. Latin is where troublemakers get put,
and it will be cut (cut — cut — what's the Latin
for that?) the following year. It was doomed
— I wasn't, surprisingly. I'm pretty proud of survival,
literacy, and scraping that O Level B in a subject
no one respected (in my world, anyway),
though I was too busy making myself throw up,
or cutting myself, to get the full benefit of an education.
"Come on, think," pleaded the teacher
(and whatever happened to him?), desperate for us
to find, through all the fimus (shit), the word for cloud.

Wonder at the Change

She's crying her eyes out
because she can't fit any more
into those star-spangled knickers.
"Tell me the truth!" she yells,
lassooing the long-suffering Steve.
"Am I fat? Am I? AM I?"
And when he replies truthfully,
"You're beautiful to me,"
she cries again. Her hot flushes
are the cause of global warming,
and her spins have slowed
so that her changes of costume
take as long as anyone else's,
and are similarly ungraceful.
But worst are the rages. She'll hurl
that tiara at the drop of a hat,
jump fifty feet on to your foot
if you say the wrong thing. Oh,
she'll still fight for a good cause;
but be very wary when with
Wonder Woman, now she's hit
the menopause.

The Gift of Chin Mu, 2346 BCE

Ch'ang O smelled sweetness and saw
a silver light in the rafters.
"What are you? Who is there?" she asked.
A voice came from a little pill,
sounding like a dream, drug or bell.
"I was given by the goddess,
Chin Mu, to your husband, Sheng I.
I confer immortality."

Ch'ang O gathered her sleeves and thought.
"Why has he not swallowed you?"
"He needed to purify,
to cleanse blood from his being,"
replied the tiny shining bead.
"He is an archer, after all
— divinely gifted, but cruel."
Ch'ang O inhaled the lucent scent
and asked, "If I am to take you,
must I undergo cleansing too?"
"No," said the pill, "For you are a
Woman, and therefore pure and clean.
You know peace and humility."
Ch'ang O smiled gently, and her gift,
a tear whitened by moonlight, fell.
She thanked the pill and ate it,
and was filled with lotuses.

Ch'ang O floated through the window
and up on a ray of the moon.
Sheng I, returning wet with blood

from his master's latest battle,
saw her and let his fury fly
as he comprehended her theft.
Arrow after barbed arrow
he hurled towards her, but Ch'ang O
shrank down to the size of a toad
and continued on her journey.

Now she dwells in peace, swimming
in the seas of the moon, singing
with the tides, spinning with starlight.

Yellow Roses on Snow

(written after visiting Sylvia Plath's grave on the fiftieth
anniversary of her death)

It's a plain grave, though thickly meringued with snow;
dark granite monolith open to the sky. The church
is old and friendly, proud with bells pealing
in glorious cascades. There is a sense of celebration
as well as mourning in the tan stone streets,
some cobbled, with views of hills, hills, hills
all covered in snow. But such a small grave,

There are several of us, strangers, women in black
lighting candles and laying the sunshine roses
(her favourite flower, her mother said)
on the grave, and mourning the dead woman
we didn't know.

Sudden sobs — it's so cold, she'll be cold,
she hated the cold. Sympathy. Chilled hands
try to warm mine. My red skirt, the blue candle
the only spots of colour save the roses,
buttery as an American sun, yellow as
a New England leaf when Autumn falls.

As if conjured, the same sun breaks out here
over the grave and us, drawing yellow and white
into a new gold. We feel relief
at the literal lightening. We had not wanted to leave
her alone, but the sun is there to warm her now.

Departing, we see knots and threads of folk
rag-rugging their way to her, heads bowed

against the bitter weather, though now the sun
is blazing, blazing on top of this blessed
hill village in Yorkshire.

Did I really think that it would be grim and dark?
That we would be given nothing here?
We were met by strength, connection
and a culmination. For us, this was pilgrimage.

Sealove

I have never spoken of my feelings for you,
partly through fear.
You could kill me with a shrugging wave
and never notice, never change a jot of rhythm.
With a sweep of air and a play of lights
you can make me cry,
yet what is a tear to you?
My weakness leaves you unchanged;
you sweep me off my feet
face-first into the push-pull of death,
startlingly salty with a rushing taste of foam,
and bits of sand and life
as tiny as I am.
Particles of crawling things,
friendly stalk-eyed aliens,
waving transparent antennae,
wriggling purposefully;
shining shell fragments or little beings,
sparkling pieces who, away from you,
are dull silt nothing.
We mites are all part of you, sharing
in your rolling might of awful beauty,
your thunder surge of crashing rage,
your great glass screens and tender tips,
the power that pulls and throbs and aches,
in the tides of my heart, birthing glory.

Rape Dreams in the Slush Pile

Of the thousand offerings, around forty
will be rape or rape/murder fantasies.
A relief, really, to find them written so very badly
— the blouses always 'flimsy', the nipples 'pouting',
'red' lips 'full', eyes 'pleading'.
She is, we hear, 'young and beautiful',
and half of them say how sad it is
as they kill her off.

The other half address her in the second person
and glory in it, and talk of destiny,
and how she won't understand, won't get it,
until (after rape, usually described as 'union'
or 'commingling') her last breath.
There may even be 'twases and 'tises in there,
and the moon will shine 'o'er' her tears and blood.

(Not like survivor poems, written with the grit
and dirt and shock and slam of it, and the
skull-fucking unbearable reality of it,
as it reverberates through their paralysed days.)

The cause of death is rarely clear, though
sometimes there's the 'glint of knife'.
This is useful in the bouncy rhyming ones,
used alongside 'end her life',
and as the unnamed woman is 'snuffed out'
the rhyme strains — 'of that there surely is no doubt'.
And language itself screams, along with
taste, women, knowledge and truth.

The fantasists make it so pretty,
her 'silk dress tattered and torn' —
and they type it up and proofread it,
and send it to me, thinking I might publish it,
lay it out carefully, name it on the contents page,
print it out a thousand times, a thousand
rapes or rape/murders, and invite them
to read it proudly at the launch.
They believe that, along with all the other myths.
They keep sending them in. And you wouldn't
believe how many use the word 'pity',
how many use the word 'love'.

Anniversaries

I am not a colossus, nor a trickster crow,
nor a man permanently dressed in SS black;
it was all her father's fault, you know.

Yes I left her, and the children too
— a minor incident. It was the father's lack
that crushed her into that cramping shoe.

Yes, I rearranged poems and excised my faults,
destroyed journals. It was mournful, not mean.
There are two human beings in the Smith vaults.

Let the youngest fox cubs play-fight and tumble.
Now she's fifty years gone, and I, fifteen.
Let the clever new bees make honey, or bumble.

The White Rose

How can we expect righteousness to prevail when there is hardly anyone willing to give himself up individually to a righteous cause? Such a fine, sunny day, and I have to go, but what does my death matter, if through us thousands of people are awakened and stirred to action?

— the last words of Sophie Scholl, member of The White Rose resistance group, before the Nazis executed her

You didn't say, one person can't make a difference.
You didn't say, there's no point in trying.
You didn't say, well, what can you do?
You didn't say that the Nazis were too powerful,
and that it was too risky.
Instead you printed your leaflets, distributed them,
and talked, and called to action;
and so they killed you.
But you had lit fires of resistance
that a cold bullet couldn't quench;
planted seeds for all of us
to follow, every new rose,
and the fires still burn
and the flowers still bloom
because you didn't do the maths
(you were just nineteen, so young)
and play the odds but instead
taught us — me — how to make a difference;
how to live and how to die,
how to light flames and grow flowers.

Passing On

Yet another of her friends died and Rae,
seventy eight, sighed as yet again
she crossed out an entry in her address book
and ironed her good black frock
and wondered why she of so many was left,
and what she could do while still here;
until presently she wasn't, and her friend Jim
crossed her entry out in his address book
and remembered her laugh, and went a bit watery
as he brushed down his well-worn dark suit;
and he felt as if he alone carried the burden
and knowledge of his generation, important work;
and then he copped it too, and, the torch passing,
someone else felt the same.

By Any Other Name

In a rich accent with roots
in the Indian continent
you say your name is Dave,
and you want to talk to me
about my phone payment plan.
Is that really your name? I ask
and you laugh, and ask me
who I'm currently with,
meaning what company —
and I'm not at all certain
what's happening here —
perhaps the call centre is located
in Birmingham, and you local,
and really called Dave
— and I'm painfully conscious
that here I'm making all kinds
of assumptions, the kinds based
on race, on accent, on colour.
Yet that call centre is probably
in Delhi or Mumbai or Bangalore,
and you've been told to tell me
your name is something English
— that's how it'll be put; as if
non-Christian names can't be
as English as I am, and the person
to whom they have been given
as rightfully of this island.
There's racism somewhere in it.
I'm pretty sure of that. No one
should be asked to change their

name, I tell Dave firmly. It's
oppressive — a form of control.
Oh? he says. The name we have
for you — is it your maiden name?

Works Xmas Do

So I'm turning up at the restaurant
in safely flattering black trousers,
my top a bit sparkly but not too flashy;
red lipstick on, as it's Xmas.
I don't look too bad in the mirror.

So I'm walking in and smiling
at the headwaiter, and I explain.
He is at a loss — there are three
different office work dos tonight.
Which one is mine? I look,

see three packed tables of
entering-into-the-spirit grins,
paper hats, jokes and the laughter
of those grateful for the undemanding
pleasantry of standard obvious jokes.

One table's a bit drunk already,
the laughter unforced now, and louder.
And at every table a balding manager
and a grey-permed, glassed supervisor;
the office beauty, and faceless clerks,

as if extras in a film chock-a-block
with clichés. And at every table
a reasonably attractive woman in her
late thirties or forties, dependable black
trousers on, slightly sparkly top,

touch of festive crimson lippy,
highlights still just enough to hide
the grey in her hair. I see this.
I look back at the headwaiter, headwaiting

politely with the bland impersonal
patience of headwaiters everywhere,
who asked which table was mine.
As if it matters.

The Insecurity of Mislocated Breasts

There's a geographical facet to colour.
Vibrant tropical reds and greens show garish
in the grey mists of England; whereas
the muted hues so fitting there are dull
to the point of sin in sunnier climates.

This comes to mind on a mediterranean beach
amid a sea of brown, lithe bodies, brown
like dark olives, like tea, like toast,
like healthy people, and I, usually (at home)
prettily pale and genteel, wandering,
a bleached out wraith, the white of a whale's belly,
and feeling the size of one.

A further shade of brown — somewhere between
earth and berry — in the thousand upturned nipples
that the sun, full of admiration for fellow
aureoled discs, gilds in honey tones.
If their breasts are ripe pomegranates
fig-nippled, then mine are turnips, peeled and boiled.
It is not coyness that keeps my top on,
nor modesty, even false. It is the very real fear
of sunburn, of returning home with Mars,
bright red and misplaced, throbbing scarlet
on each moony globe.

Next year I'll holiday somewhere where
jackets are advisable, and the locals remark
on the heat if it gets to short sleeves and socklessness.
Or else I'll just remember the sunblock and fake tan.

Vital

Bare your breast, Colette,
and be vilified, castigated
and pelted with detritus
as you act out love and drama.

Open your heart, Colette
as you wrench off the old love
and regard the new players
with the clear mournful eyes of a cat.

Follow your desires, Colette,
for the louche playboy
for the aristocratic androgyne
for the flawless young dear.

Bare your breast, open your heart and follow
your desires, Colette — and sharpen your pen.

Mental Illness

One tries to explain with imagery:
you have a giant weight on you;
you can't move; people are all around you,
screeching that you're useless and disgusting.

Look, it's like trying to escape from
the mad axeman who'll torture and kill you,
but the mad axeman is life and the world
and also yourself.

It doesn't quite work. It won't take the form,
breaks up and ruins the meter, won't submit
to rhyme:
today you find that you can't do
a thing but cry upon the loo.

No. I can't explain. And you?
Can you understand anyway?
Will you hold me anyway?

Good Job

It is 1986 and I work in an unemployment benefit office.
An office full of meanness and gossip.
There is no coffee, no water, just the clack
of machinery and bitter jaws. The banter is painful.
It's kept obvious and intolerant.
Every single woman here is on a diet.
I weigh 140 lbs and hate myself.
We wrestle papers and the public.
I am paid the same amount as those on the other side
of the counter, though I don't get kicked down
the way they do.
I don't fit in. I have never known how to have fun,
'a laugh'. I have a crush on the most unpleasant
bloke here. A womaniser, a show off.
Nothing comes of it, thankfully.
Dead air, I can give and take nothing.
At 17, everything I say comes out wrong.
My desperation is a silent clenched fist.
I have fallen into the wrong life.

It is 2006 and I am in a studio in an old mill.
Sometimes soft music plays; usually there is silence
apart from the scratch-sweep of brushes and palette
knives, the splosh of brushes in water.
I weigh 200 lbs and lie naked on a swathe of red satin
draped over a couch. Thirty strangers watch me
pose under spotlights.
I am paid decent money for the first time in my life.
I am becoming art:
'The Little Face' in one painting, an erotic torso

in another. An ancient Mycenean goddess in conté crayons.
A charcoal Valkyrie. Wild flowing lines in biro.
My eyes are opened to the possibility of myriad
reflections, of self-image as a creative choice.
I am many models and all of them real.
I could be a necklace or a sea-creature or a texture.
See, on this cartridge paper, my hair dance in pastels.
I have not found my permanent installation yet; I will travel
with myself first, make an exhibition of myself in public.
Not selfish but self-ful, at last. Then and only then
I will be able to give myself and open, to pick up
a brush or a pen, and hold out my hands.

Lying on the Ground for the First Time in Thirty Years

First time in the garden. Oh god,
that toast-crack sound of summer grass under me,
that familar but long absent prickling and unevenness.
A thousand tiny creatures say hello and start
to kiss my legs. The smell, hot earth and plants;
the ground a breathing lover, squashing
my breasts and touching, touching,
our hips jarring against each other.

Next time, on the beach. My happy place.
I have wiggled my toes in sand a thousand times
but now I lie down and again, it is a breathing, living thing
kissing my back and shoulders. I turn over
and am glittering with fragments of mica,
dirty with brownish sand. I sit up, brush it off;
lie again and get more on me. Wriggle,
wriggle, wiggle, wiggle. Lose myself.

Sit up, legs spread, pat the sand, sweep the sand,
write in it. My partner offers, meaning no sarcasm
or reproof, to buy me a bucket and spade.
No. The reason being that I remember the harsh edges
of cheap plastic, the disappointing edifices.
I play like a baby, not a toddler.
I rub sand on my operation scars and smile.

I have learned to crawl, fall and lie.
Anything is possible now.
Imagine me running into the sea, laughing
the way the very small do, their legs
taking them wherever their eyes want to go.

Look At All The Women

Look at that woman breastfeeding in public!
I think it's absolutely disgusting

the way people give her a hard time.

Look at that lass in a minidress!
Whore! Slag! Bitch! Slut!

are just some of the things she'll be called
by prejudiced strangers.

Look at that grandmother!
A lot of support is needed

from her for all her friends and relatives,
but she still finds time to lead a vibrant, balanced life.

Look at that campaigner!
She should get to the kitchen,

have a glass of wine and put her feet up,
later on, after standing up for us all.

Look at that woman writer!
It'll be all flowers, dresses and chocolates

at her many literary award ceremonies.

Look at that sister!
She's arguing with her siblings again

which, done with affection and a willingness
to compromise, is a really useful life skill.

Look at that stay-at-home mother!
She doesn't work, of course

apart from 24 hours a day, seven days a week
doing one of the most important jobs there is.

Look at that woman scientist!
She's outside her natural environment

analysing soil samples from the planet Mars.

Look at me!
Ill and unable to work again

but still making people laugh, and still giving
the best hugs in Manchester.

Look at that cleaner!
The lowest of the low

will sneer at her, as she makes our lives pleasanter
for a pittance.

Look at that daughter!
Disappointing, really

that she still has so much sexism to face.

Look at that lesbian!
You can tell what she needs

— equality, and recognition of
her voice that enriches us all.

Look at that schoolgirl!
They shouldn't be educated

differently from boys.

Look at all the women!
What a waste of time

life would be without them.

About the Author

Cathy Bryant was born in 1967 in Hampshire, but moved around a lot as a child. At the age of nine she moved to Lancashire and loved it; at the age of eighteen she moved to Manchester and settled there. Among the many jobs she has done are: civil servant, nursery assistant and life model.

She submitted her first pieces of work to magazines only because her best friend blackmailed her into it, seven years ago. She did it to prove to him that no one would want to publish them — and she was delighted to be wrong.

Cathy has won ten literary awards, including the Bulwer-Lytton Fiction Prize in 2012 and a Creative Literary Futures Gold Award, and has also blogged for the *Huffington Post*. Her work has been published all over the world in such publications as *Third Wednesday*, *The Rialto* website and *Popshot*. She co-edited the anthologies *Best of Manchester Poets Vols. 1, 2 and 3* and her first book, *Contains Strong Language and Scenes of a Sexual Nature* was published in 2010.

Working around her disabilities and health problems, Cathy writes whenever she can. Her current projects include a Jane Austen themed comedy novel, and a possible e-book about how to win writing competitions.

The oddest thing that ever happened to Cathy was being struck by lightning and bitten by a poisonous spider on the same day, at a wedding in a field in Tennessee.

Mother's Milk Books
is an independent press, founded and managed by
at-home mother, Dr Teika Bellamy.

The aim of the press is to publish high-quality, beautiful books
that normalize breastfeeding, empower parents, provide
positive role models and encourage creativity.
The annual Mother's Milk Books Writing Prize, which
welcomes poetry and prose from both adults and children,
runs from September to mid-January.
Mother's Milk Books also produces and sells art
and poetry prints, as well as greetings cards.
For more information about the press, and to make purchases
from the online store,
please visit: www.mothersmilkbooks.com